MW01289131

Psychic Horizons Workbooks and Workouts

How to Develop your Intuition

Carole Anne Somerville

Copyright 2016 Carole A Somerville
All rights reserved. No part of this publication may be reproduced, stored in or introduced into a retrieval system, or transmitted, in any form, or by any means (electronic, mechanical, photocopying, recording, or otherwise) without the prior written permission of the copyright owner.

ISBN-13:
978-1537103778

ISBN-10:
1537103776

Spiritual Development Workbooks

Nurture your Mind, Body, Soul & Spirit
Tap into your Psychic Self
Build your Spiritual Muscles

"The more you trust your intuition, the more empowered you
become, the stronger you become, and the happier you become."
~ Gisele Bundchen

Contents:

This Workbook is devoted to helping you recognise your intuitive responses to gain a better understanding of yourself and how you can use your intuition in your daily life.

I would recommend that you start a Journal before you begin reading this book in which you can record results of exercises, dreams and intuitive experiences.

I hope you will enjoy this fun and insightful journey.

One

What is Intuition?

How do we recognise intuition?

Intuition can be described in many ways. There is often an air of mystery surrounding intuitive/psychic feelings and these are seldom discussed during casual conversations. Yet we use our intuition on a daily basis; this sixth sense often complementing our judgement and decision making processes. – You probably use your intuition more than you realise.

Intuitive feelings stem from our subconscious ... our inner self ... from deep inside and because these feelings come to us in a flash and vanish just as quickly, it can sometimes be difficult to grasp onto them. Since they don't come from analysis or rational thought ... they are feelings or thoughts that appear from out of nowhere ... it can be hard for some people to trust, rely on, recognise our justify their intuitive responses and often they are dismissed as meaningless.

How do we Recognise Intuition?

Intuitive responses come to us in many different ways: sudden thoughts, flashes of insight, a difficult to explain 'feeling that something isn't right', hairs standing on the back of your neck, tingles down the spine ... Intuition is often talked about as an inner knowing or gut feeling. Thoughts or feelings that suddenly come into our conscious that don't relate to anything we are thinking about or experiencing at the time.

So there is nothing rational about intuition and this makes it hard for us to explain these feelings. They are something that comes to us in a flash from hidden realms within. Think of the word 'intuition' ... 'in' from inside ... 'tuition' ... tuition from our inner-selves.

A hunch is not emotional but there is a 'feeling' aspect to intuitive responses. This response that we describe as a gut feeling is what draws attention to our conscious mind that there is something going on, beyond what we are thinking or seeing.

Intuitive messages come from the soul. Intuition speaks to everyone differently so a good way to find out how your intuition speaks to you is to test it on small things at first like: 'what kind of day am I going to have today?' ... how do you intuitively feel about this? By the end of the day you will know whether your intuition got it right.

This workbook will include exercises to help you tune into your intuition. The more you use your sixth sense, the more you will start to recognise your intuitive responses, the results through following these and how your intuition strengthens. You will start to trust your intuition more and this will allow it to develop even further.

What Intuition is Not

Intuition is not daydreaming. Intuition is not imagination. Intuition is not hope.

Intuition is not wishful thinking. – Joseph, for instance, believed his intuition was telling him that he would be promoted. He applied for an interview for a higher job and told everyone he was the one who'd be offered the position. When the job went to another colleague he found it hard to hide his disappointment. Later he realised it hadn't been intuition that he'd been acting on but wishful thinking.

Intuition is not Ego. - Amelia believed her intuition was telling her that she would one day become a famous medium. She did platform work and got good feedback. When she excitedly decided to arrange an evening mediumship and charged high prices for this event, few people turned up. Feedback on the night was disappointing. She was crushed that the idea was a failure. When she examined her behaviour later Amelia realised it had not been true intuition that she was acting on but her ego's desire for her to be rich and famous.

Developing your Intuition

You might think you aren't very intuitive or you have had no psychic experiences but maybe you have without realising it. Ask yourself for instance whether you've ever had a feeling of deja vu? Or have you occasionally found yourself looking at the telephone seconds before it started ringing?

Can you sometimes tell what people are going to say before they utter the words? Or has an impulse ever led you to change plans or to change the route of a journey, perhaps because of an uneasy feeling about continuing as arranged?

Intuition can show itself in many ways including: Telepathy, Clairvoyance, Mediumship, Dowsing, Dreams and Precognition. Intuition in its many forms helps people to open their minds to such possibilities. Some areas you may already have heard about, some might be new to you. Some will interest you more than others. There are many different exercises and experiments that can help you test your psychic power and develop your intuition.

Developing your Intuition will help enrich your life by helping to:

* put you in touch with your subconscious
* feel more in control of your destiny

* enhance your personal relationships
* heal yourself and others
* enjoy a more relaxed style of living

The first step to increasing your mental powers and spiritual understanding is to believe in yourself and believe in your psychic abilities.

Rid yourself of any notion that only 'special' people are psychic. That is not so. Everyone is psychic and pursuing exercises to develop your intuition will help put you in touch with your Higher Self.

Learning to Quieten Your Mind

How much time do you spend each day alone? The answer to this will of course depend on your obligations towards others. However, if you want to tap into your inner resources, it's important to start devoting at least 15 minutes a day to yourself. You will need to find somewhere peaceful where outside distractions are at a minimum; a place where you can feel relaxed and comfortable.

To learn how to trust your intuition, you must learn how to become completely relaxed. You may already be familiar with relaxation techniques but if you are new to this, have patience. Try some breathing and relaxation exercises to help you quieten your mind.

The more you do this, the easier it will be to quieten your mind, ready for your psychic development to begin.

Everyone Is Psychic

Everyone has some degree of psychic ability.

People depend on their intuition sometimes without even realising it. They might make what seems like a lucky guess after a flash of intuition. Learning how to meditate can be the first step towards enhancing spirituality. This will help strengthen power of concentration and increase psychic energy.

Eventually there will be no need to test your psychic power or intuitive responses. Just believing there is a whole new dimension to your world that is psychic and spiritual will be enough and instead of 'testing' your intuition or psychic power your aim will be to develop your innate abilities.

What are the Differences between Intuition and Psychic Ability?

Psychic ability and intuition are closely linked. Intuition is a feeling or instinct, a 'knowing' yet not through analysis. Thousands of years ago man relied on their intuition to protect themselves. They would sense where there was danger, where animals may be lurking and whether or not they posed a threat. Intuition can help give us a first impression of someone we meet … a gut instinct or feeling … and whether or not we might trust them.

Intuition is a tool developed out of necessity for survival. Psychic ability can be another survival tool that goes deeper than intuition. Psychic information is more detailed than intuitive information. It might begin with an intuitive reaction but a psychic will focus on this response to receive more specific detail. Information provided might come through clairvoyance, clairsentience, claircognizance or clairaudience. Psychic ability can be a way of receiving information from outside yourself … sensing atmosphere of a room, picking up information from touch (psychometry) for instance, whereas intuition is a form of instinct: a gut feeling that comes from within.

Psychic Workout ... Thinking about Intuition

Write down in your journal the first thing that comes to your mind when you see the following question:

If intuition was an image, what would it be?

Now consider the image that came to you and what this might say about your understanding of intuition.

(Example of above exercise from one of our students: I saw a closed door. What this said to me was that my intuition was closed to me. I don't have a connection with my Higher Self but I do believe that my intuition is behind that closed door and through working on my spiritual development, the door will open and I will connect with my deeper instincts).

What are the Clairs?

Psychic ability is sometimes referred to as the sixth sense and this consists of five psychic senses that correspond to the five physical senses. These are often referred to as the 'clairs': clairvoyance, clairaudience, clairsentience, clairalience and clairgustance.

Clairvoyance – Clear Sight – The ability to see, through visions and dreams. Some psychics can see things with their eyes open. Some receive images behind closed eyes.
Clairaudience – Clear hearing – hearing sounds through the psychic senses. These can be words, music and other noises that cannot be accounted for in the environment.
Clairsentience – Clear feeling – this might be experienced as a tingling, a slight coolness or a breeze wafting across your face. You might 'feel' a change in the energy around you.
Claralience – Clear smelling – occasionally you might smell something that cannot be accounted for in the physical world around you ... cakes when no one is baking, a flowery scent or cigar/cigarette smoke.

Clairgustance – Clear tasting – Spirit can sometimes provide us with tastes of food that might remind us of past loved ones.
Claircognizance is a 'clear knowing'. This is like an intuitive response, a sudden knowing without being able to explain why.

Psychic Workout ... Exercises to heighten Intuition

Enhance your inner vision:

Any exercise that uses visualisation is good for helping to strengthen your clairvoyant ability as this is also developing your imagination. This is the tool that our Higher Self, Guides or spirit use to send us information. The more we are able to use our visual imagination the easier it is for us to receive clear intuitive/psychic images.

Enhance your powers of visualisation:

Close your eyes and imagine you are holding seven different coloured balloons: blue, yellow, green, violet, red, indigo and orange. Now visualise letting go of the balloons, one by one, beginning with the blue balloon. Watch the balloon float up to the sky and then release the yellow one. Again watch it float up to the sky before releasing the next one.

If you aren't used to visualisation exercises this might take a lot of concentration and it may be hard to visualise the balloons or see the colours. Keep practising.

Exercise to open your Third Eye Chakra

Imagine you have a Third Eye in the middle of your forehead. Now visualise the eyelid on your Third Eye opening. Try to visualise this regularly. Often when using psychic ability if you find it hard to actually imagine what you need to, setting the intention is sufficient. As you try to visualise your Third Eye opening, set the intention that you are also opening the centre of your clairvoyant abilities. At the end of the exercise imagine (or set the intention) that your eyelid on your Third Eye is closing.

Exercise to enhance your inner hearing

Relax for a few moments. Now imagine you are listening to the radio and you have sent in a request to the DJ to play a song that is meaningful for you at this particular time. Listen to the song that is being played. Listen to the words even if you only hear a few then write down in your Journal why you think your intuition chose this particular song for you.

Exercise to enhance your awareness of physical sensations

When going about your daily business start paying attention to your body. Notice the way you breathe or when you feel tingles down your spine. A sad feeling or heavy heart can be your body's way of telling you that something is wrong. Trust your intuitive bodily reactions as sometimes our bodies can sense things our minds have yet to recognise.

What should you do now?

Arrange it so you can have 15 minutes a day to yourself ... if your day is full the moment you get up in the morning, get up 15 minutes earlier. Use this time to practice the above exercises on enhancing your powers of intuition.

Points to Ponder

Intuition is a gut feeling, a 'knowing' without analysis or reasoning. A chief executive decided to turn down a big contract because he did not feel it would be right for the Company. Others questioned his decision as it could not be validated at the time by evidence. It later turned out that the deal had several loopholes which would have been costly had they agreed on it.

Which other situations /conditions might a business executive rely on their intuition?

Two

How to Develop your Intuition and Enhance Psychic Sensitivity

Intuition in your everyday life

What does it mean to be psychic and how can you enhance your intuition and psychic abilities?

Everyone, it is said, has some degree of psychic ability. With the stresses and pressures of modern day living, it is often difficult for us to pause and focus on our subconscious. Those who use their psychic abilities, centre their attention on their inner-being, sensing, seeing and sometimes hearing spiritual messages.

Some psychics will have been aware of their abilities in childhood, some will say their psychic gifts are inherited whereas others will develop a psychic leaning later in life.

With so much emphasis on the material-world, psychics are sometimes viewed with a sense of wonder and sometimes, sensibly, with suspicion and caution. What a lot of people don't realise, however, is that everyone can develop their psychic talents or powers of intuition, if they want to.

Are You Intuitive?

You might have had intuitive or psychic experiences which you've dismissed as coincidence, luck or imagination. Perhaps there have been times when you've known who was on the other end of the phone as soon as it began to ring. Or maybe you felt you had to get in touch with someone to find they were ill or in need of help. Many of us have intuitive experiences without realisng them for what they are. The psychic will recognise their instinctive responses, focus on them and strive to develop these talents further.

Everyone has the potential to develop their intuition and psychic potential and to use this to enhance their personal, professional and spiritual lives. There are methods you can use to open up your mind, develop your spiritual powers and tap into your psychic-self. Your intention, however, must always be good and full of love for your fellow man. Remember the law of karma: as you sow, so shall you reap!

Intuition Defined

The dictionary describes intuition as: 'the immediate knowing or learning of something without the conscious use of reasoning; instantaneous perception.'

Intuition is also called ESP by some, or a 'sixth sense'. Intuition is not really a sense on its own but it is more an extension of our normal five senses. Intuition goes beyond these and is often experienced as a 'knowing' or a gut feeling. Intuitive feelings can also cause physical symptoms such as tingling down the spine, goose bumps, butterflies in the stomach or a heavy heart. Intuition is a feeling that seems to come out of nowhere. That "I don't know how, I just know," sensation.

I particularly like Carl Jung's description of intuition as an 'aspect of consciousness that allows us to see round corners.'

In ancient times when man relied on instinct for hunting, our intuition will have been much more powerful. Our ancestors may have used their intuition to help them find water, the best hunting grounds or the safest places to spend the night. Slowly through the Ages we had less need of our intuition to survive on a daily basis and that inner knowing has become dulled. It still lies dormant, however, and it is possible to learn to use it and trust it again. You might look on your intuition as a powerful gift to yourself should you choose to develop it.

So, intuition is not psychic ability or mediumship. Everyone has a degree of intuition and it can be developed like every skill, through practice. To be an intuitive person you need to be honest with yourself. You need to distinguish between true intuitive information and wishful thinking. Practice is the only way to develop intuition. All you need is an open mind, a sense of adventure and your Journal to help you keep track of your intuitive hits and misses. I can promise you that the more you work on your intuition, the more hits there will be than misses.

Trust and Intuition

When learning how to trust your intuition, it is important to clear your mind and spend times in quiet so you become more aware of your inner-self. You can't always hear your inner voice in noisy environments, when life is chaotic or when you have worries and other thoughts running through your mind. You may need to find ways to drown out your inner critic, calm all those thoughts that are whirling through your head and create space in your thinking. There are a number of ways you can do this and this book will provide you with a few.

Reiki has been a big help to me for getting in touch with my intuition. It has helped open me up to Divine Energy, to invite this energy into my 'self' and world every day as well as connecting me with my intuition on a deeper level.

When we listen to our intuition and follow intuitive guidance we are able to connect with our inner wisdom and this helps us follow our passions. Intuition can be felt in so many different ways such as a sudden feeling of lightness or dizziness that's like a spiritual excitement that makes you know something is very right for you. Intuitive responses can cause goose bumps, shivers down the spine or tingles all over your body. Or an inexplicable feeling of joy which makes you 'know' you just have to follow a certain direction. Intuition can be just a plain and simple 'inner knowing'.

Once you learn how to recognise your intuition you will discover you use it all the time. Of course we can make mistakes but that helps us learn. I recently for instance agreed to arrangements then instantly felt it was wrong for me. I was tempted to pull out but didn't want to let anyone down. Yet for days felt it wasn't going to go right. When the time came, the event wasn't as it had been described and there were costs that hadn't been revealed ... I should have trusted my intuition and next time I feel that way I WILL trust it. Generally intuition plays a vital role in my life. I meditate regularly, use my psychic skills every day (which enhances intuition) and I'm always listening to my inner voice (I can hear it in quiet surroundings but even in noisy ones too). This is a wonderful journey and I hope a one that you will enjoy embarking on too.

How to Develop your Psychic Ability

Psychic ability is the ability to see and hear beyond the material; to 'tune into' life's secrets. By developing your psychic powers, you are in fact, expanding your mind and perceptions and by being more aware of your connection with the Universe, you can learn how to interpret and express your inner truth. Nature has her own language. All creatures and objects have their own vibration; a 'language' of their own. Psychic ability is the skill to tune into the language of the Universe and its life energy.

It is believed that everyone has some degree of psychic ability, even if they aren't aware of this. Have you ever found yourself acting on intuition and then being grateful later, that you trusted your instincts? Psychic ability can be developed from intuitive responses and again, some people will see results surprisingly quickly whilst others will have to be more patient.

In order to develop your intuition, look after your body. Be wise about what you eat. Cut down on sugar, white flour and coffee. Eat fresh fruits and vegetables daily and exercise regularly. These will help clear the body and ease meditation.

Intuition and Decision Making

Decision making can be a mix of intuition and indeed experience and common sense but instinct can play a role in decision making.

Our intuitive responses come from our subconscious as our subconscious might find links between what is occurring now and patterns from our past experiences. We may not recall these experiences or the details of these experiences but they will be filed away in our subconscious to draw on whenever we might need it. Our subconscious can rapidly draw on past lessons or make a quick link with the Universal Conscious to send us messages of wisdom which we receive as intuitive responses. These messages come as a hunch, an inner voice or just a 'feeling' that some of the options or solutions we are considering aren't right for us.

Psychic Workout ... Intuition and Making Decisions

Exercise to link into your intuition when making decisions

When making a decision: choose a quiet place where can be comfortable and won't be disturbed
Write down the decision you have to make
Make a list of all possible options and alternatives
Make a list of pros and cons in relation to these options
Now close the book you have been writing in or turn the paper over so you can't see the words
Close your eyes
Take a few deep breaths
Think of someone you love and allow that loving feeling to fill your heart and soul
Say the word 'love' three times in your mind (this will open your Heart Chakra)
Now think of the decision you have to make and notice what comes instantly to your mind –
This will be the decision that comes from your heart and your intuition rather than through analysis ... what you 'feel' you should do for the best.

Another good way to make 'intuitive' decisions is to follow the above procedure, writing the pros and cons of the choices available. Then sleep on it and allow your subconscious mind to work on the issue while you are sleeping. In the morning, ask yourself what you feel you should do ... your Higher Self will reply.

Meditation and Psychic Abilities

Meditation is one of the best ways to start developing intuition and in turn, your psychic ability. Choose quiet times and peaceful places. Find an object to focus on: a gem or crystal, a tarot card or a candle flame. Relax. It might take some time before you start seeing images in your mind's eye, but persevere. With patience and practice, the Universal Energy will start to flow. Quiet times of meditation will help you tune into your intuition through helping your mind become more aware of your inner self and information received from your subconscious.

Meditation in Daily Life

Many people don't realise how it is possible to meditate when doing simple tasks that don't require a lot of thought such as washing the dishes, gardening, cleaning and housework. While you are doing these tasks, your mind can often drift off into a world of its own. You may even be in a meditative state without realising it. One way to clear your mind of intrusive thoughts is to focus on a detail of the task you are performing. Start by focusing on your breathing. Then, for instance, gaze with a soft focus at the bubbles as you wash the dishes. Keep your gaze on the bubbles and when thoughts come into your mind, acknowledge these, release them and refocus on your breathing. Clearing your mind helps you become more in tune with your intuition.

Intuition in your Everyday Life

You may already rely on your intuition regularly as you go about your daily affairs.

Often things just pop into our heads out of nowhere and after having acted on them we look back and think: how weird I knew I would need that item at some point today. Or how strange that

I sensed I would have to do something or check on someone, even before I was aware of it.

Or if we did not act on that 'spontaneous thought' we might wish we'd trusted our hunches when we had the chance because it could have made a big difference to the consequences of the day.

Instances of trusting your hunches include:

* Suddenly thinking of picking up groceries when coming home from work to find a housemate had been going to ask you to get these but forgot.
* Stocking up on extra food a day before unexpected visitors call by.
* Calling a friend when they come to your mind to find they've been thinking of you or they need someone to talk to.
* Throwing a raincoat in your bag as you walk out the door despite there being no sign of rain and having it handy during a later rainstorm.
* Tidying the house just before in-laws drop by unexpectedly.
* Clearing out a cupboard on a whim to find an item you had been looking for the day before.
* Having an uneasy feeling something is wrong and when checking discovering you were right to trust your instincts.

Who's Calling?

When you receive a text message or phone call, your instant reaction may be to wonder who is sending you the text or trying to get in touch with you. Sometimes you just know who it's going to be before opening the message.

Over the next week before responding when you receive a text message alert, or before answering your phone, try to intuitively sense who it is that is calling. Make a note of your responses in your Journal. – How often do you get it right?

What Kind of Day?

When you wake in the morning spend a few moments trying to sense what kind of day you are likely to have. Will everything go smoothly? Will there be challenges to overcome? Will people be cooperative? Will someone be argumentative?
At the end of the day think about your earlier feelings and note in your Journal how you sensed some things correctly or otherwise. Think about your intuitive responses, how these came to you and which ones you might trust.

Intuition and Nature

Getting out in nature and in touch with Mother Earth is another good way to develop your intuition. Being in the woods, the countryside, a park, by the sea connects you with Nature's energy and this helps calm you and ground you.

As you are walking, standing or sitting outdoors, think of an issue or dilemma that you've recently been trying to resolve. Focus on the question for a short while then let it go and simply enjoy your surroundings.

As you walk if you are drawn to a stone, a twig, a leaf or any object that catches your eye, pick it up, hold it, close your eyes and try to feel its energy. Again ask the question that was on your mind and if you see an image in your head, a word or get a feeling, trust in this insight that nature is giving you about your question.

Intuition and Dreams

How often have you heard the phrase 'let me sleep on it?' When we sleep, we dream. Our dreams help to provide insight and solutions that evade our conscious minds. We may wake up with a sudden knowing of how to solve a problem or of what we need to do that day. We might not remember dreaming but we could suddenly feel inspired the moment we wake, to take certain action. Often when we act on those first thoughts of the morning, we find we have been guided to do what was right for us at that time. This is our intuition at work. Our intuition speaks to us through our dreams.

Psychic Workout ... Remembering your Dreams

Some people easily recall their dreams, some will say they 'never' dream. We all dream but we don't all 'remember' our dreams. I find that I have phases where I remember my dreams vividly then I can go for months knowing I have dreamed but I am unable to 'latch onto them' with my conscious mind. I also find that if I wake up and go back to sleep in the night, I am more likely to recall my dreams during those early hours of the morning.

How important to you find the following in remembering your dreams? For each statement, respond with 0 – Not important at all, 1 – Reasonably important, 2 – Very important, 3 – Highly important

1 You remember dreams more when an alarm clock wakes you

2 You remember dreams more after reading novels or watching TV dramas/films

3 You remember dreams more when you have been creative during the day

4 You remember dreams depending on which time of night you wake up

5 You remember dreams more easily if you instantly try to recall them when waking

6 You need to believe you can remember your dreams

6 Suggesting a theme of a dream before going to sleep helps you recall your dreams in the morning

7 Feelings when you wake up, help you to remember your dreams

9 You need to write down your dreams immediately or you forget them

Now take another look at the above and your scores. Numbers 1 to 3 reflect how outside influences or daytime activities help you recall your dreams. Numbers 4 to 9 reflect on the importance of being 'aware' of your dreaming self and what you can do to help you remember your dreams.

If you don't remember your dreams often, thinking about the above can help you develop strategies to help you recall your dreams. For instance if number 1 is important and you want to remember your dreams, you might set your alarm to wake you every two hours during the night. The moment you wake, try to recall your dreams and write them down in a dream journal before going back to sleep. If number 2 is important, you might spend time before going to sleep, reading a novel to stimulate your dreaming mind and powers of dream recall.

Grounding and Shielding

Grounding and shielding is recommended for use before giving intuitive readings but also in your everyday life to protect your aura and psychic self. Its purpose is to allow you to be open to receive information through your intuition or psychically while remaining closed to the energy draining effect which can take place when:

- You are in crowded situations (absorbing other people's energies without being consciously aware of it

- You open yourself to people who are in need

- You are in environments where some traumatic event or chaos occurred where the energy remains distorted or powerful

Remember too, that everyone is capable of absorbing energy from people around them particularly when they are anxious, drained, upset or even angry. Nine times out of ten they won't be doing this deliberately, as, like breathing, this occurs at a subconscious level.

When giving intuitive readings, linking with people intuitively during conversations, doing volunteer work or giving healing, there is a two-way link. You may want or need to help people at times when you feel emotionally or physically drained, or even during a crisis. Taking energy from others, or passing on negative energy to them, isn't something you might do consciously but be aware that it does happen and this is another reason why it is important to ground and shield.

Grounding and protecting is something you should do regularly to help calm you, ground you and protect you. Do this too whenever you feel the need. It is self-administered and helps to keep you balanced. You can't overdose on it.

Grounding connects you to the earth's energy and helps keep you stabilised. It can also help prevent you from depleting your own energy. Bring your attention to your feet and imagine them being planted firmly into the ground. Visualise roots growing from your feet, into the earth. See them growing thickly and deeply. Now as you breathe in, you are drawing earth-energy up through your roots. As you breathe out, you are sending your roots deeper into the ground below. Focus on this exercise for a few minutes and this will strengthen your connection with the earth.

You can also use gemstones to help ground you. Wear these or keep them close by. Hematite reflects negative energy back to its source, Black Tourmaline and Black Obsidian will absorb negative energy. Smokey Quartz helps ground, protect and uplift your own energy.

To protect your aura, you might imagine a bubble of white, pure light surrounding you from head to toe and set the intention that this energy bubble protects you from any negativity that is around you or being directed your way. You might also call upon the Angels (depending on your beliefs) to help protect you. Ask that the Angels protect and guide you and remove any burdens to allow your creativity and intuition to flow freely. You might say a prayer to Archangel Michael, calling upon his healing presence to protect and guide you. Ask that He protects you from negative energies and assists you on your path.

What should you do now?

Continue to make a note of all your intuitive experiences and the results of Intuitive Exercises in your journal. Date your entries so you can look back in the future to see how you have developed over time. Start keeping a Dream Journal. Try to analyse your dreams. Read books and do some research on dream analysis.

Points to Ponder:

Do you pay attention to your intuition?
How intuitive do you feel you are?
Have you relied on intuition in daily life without realising this?

How can intuition play a part in decision making? Think of a decision-making situation where you have used both facts and intuition to help you analyse the situation.

... Make a note of your thoughts in your Journal.

Three

Intuition and your Chakras

How to enhance your intuition through balancing your Chakras

There are seven major energy centres in the body and these are called Chakras.

Chakra is a Sanskrit word meaning wheel and Chakras can be seen to be coloured energy vortexes – spinning wheels - within our body.

Each Chakra is linked with a physical organ, aspects of your emotional well-being and a different layer in the spiritual aura. They are a part of the consciousness or soul and they are a way in which our Higher Self is connected to our physical being.

Many Reiki practitioners use Chakras to focus and direct Universal energy. Energy is absorbed by the Chakras and distributed within the body.

Through working with and understanding the different Chakras, you too, can attune your own and other people's mental, physical, emotional and spiritual energies.

The seven main Chakras are:

- Root Chakra
- Sacral Chakra
- Solar Plexus Chakra
- Heart Chakra
- Throat Chakra
- Third Eye Chakra

- Crown Chakra

Root Chakra and Intuition

Your Root Chakra is the first Chakra, located at the base of the spine and is the root of your whole being: your connection with your body. Your body is the physical home for all life's experiences and the storehouse for all your emotions, mental observations and memories. Negative emotional and intellectual experiences can manifest in the body as ill health or aches and pains. You can learn, through your intuition, how to understand the messages your body is sending you. You will begin to intuit how emotional and spiritual issues are revealing themselves through your body. When this Chakra is blocked you may not feel grounded, your energy is weak and you might feel nervous and highly strung. You might fear change, feel bored or lethargic. You may turn to food and material items for a sense of comfort or security which could lead to greed or overabundance.

Questions to ask yourself to check this Chakra is balanced:

Do I feel connected with nature?
Do I live a balanced existence (equal balance between work and play, me-time and social time)?
Do I feel emotionally secure?
Is there stability in my life?
Am I content?
Do I feel safe?
Am I able to make good decisions?
Do I set healthy boundaries?
Am I grounded?

The more 'yes' answers to the above the more likely it is your Root Chakra is balanced.

If your Root Chakra is blocked, you might: Add regular exercise to your daily routine; go for long walks in the countryside; listen to music that has a deep beat and this will help you feel a link with Mother Earth; ground yourself through the grounding exercise in Chapter two of this book; carry red gemstones (i.e. ruby, red jasper, garnet) in your pocket or wallet.

Sacral Chakra and Intuition

Your Sacral Chakra is located just below your naval. This Chakra is linked with your emotional body and offers the spiritual lessons of creativity, intuition, empathy and intimacy. The Sacral Chakra links you with your passions, your dreams, ambitions and fantasies. When this Chakra is blocked, it can lead to emotional outbursts and control issues in relationships. When emotions are high, this can block intuitive feelings. Conversely, intuition can be enhanced through creativity and through feeling good about yourself and your relationships.

Questions to ask yourself to check this Chakra is balanced:

Am I able to express my feelings in close relationships?
Can I relax and go with the flow in relationships?
Am I able to honour my highest self through my relationships?
Am I learning all I can about myself through my relationships?
Am I able to recognise and release feelings of control and jealousy?
Am I in touch with my dreams?
Do I feel there is a good connection between my intuition and creativity?
Am I nurturing of myself and others?
Do I trust my gut instinct?
Do I have a good sense of humour?
Am I able to express myself creatively?

The more 'yes' answers to the above the more likely it is your Sacral Chakra is balanced.

If your Sacral Chakra is blocked, you might: Watch a romantic movie; spend a day cooking for your family or sign up for a cookery course; get creative; carry orange gemstones (i e. orange Kyanite or Amber) in your pocket or your wallet.

Solar Plexus Chakra and Intuition

Your Solar Plexus is located in the upper abdomen. This Chakra is associated with feelings of confidence, self-worth and your sense of responsibility. When this Chakra is balanced you have high levels of self-respect and will feel at peace with yourself. You will feel cheerful, flexible and calm in mind. A healthy self-esteem is vital to enhancing your intuition. Low self-esteem makes you more judgemental of yourself, you feel disconnected with the world around you and out of touch with your intuition.

If the Solar Plexus Chakra is blocked you may have problems controlling your ego or recognising when it is controlling you, you might lack confidence, feel angry, isolated, frustrated, depressed or doubtful.

Questions to ask yourself to check this Chakra is balanced:

Do I feel I have a healthy self-esteem?
Am I able to see the good in most situations?
Is my emotional life fulfilling?
Am I sociable?
Do I try to keep my thoughts positive?
Is my cup half full?
Do I try to go with the flow?
Do I include activities I enjoy into my daily routines?
Do I help others through a genuine and sincere desire to be of service?

The more 'yes' answers to the above the more likely it is your Solar Plexus Chakra is balanced.

If your Solar Plexus Chakra is blocked, you might: Spend time outdoors in sunlight; stand still in the open air and breathe in the Sun's energy; fill in crosswords and mind puzzles; start a new hobby or pick up an old one. Carry yellow gemstones (i.e. topaz or amber) in your pocket or wallet.

Heart Chakra and Intuition

The Heart Chakra, as its name suggests, is associated with issues of the heart and your ability to feel love. This is your Centre for unconditional love. Emotions held within your heart can bring you immense joy but also great pain. You receive intuitive messages from your heart in the form of a 'knowing' or 'feeling' that cannot be explained. A working mother, for instance, might suddenly feel there is something wrong with her child and has a strong urge to contact her child-minder. When your Heart Chakra is balanced, this strengthens the connection between heart and brain so when sudden insights pop into your mind you are more likely to accept these without analysis.

When the Heart Chakra is blocked, you might feel resentful, unloving, unkind, lonely, betrayed, jealous and unforgiving of self or others.

Questions to ask yourself to check this Chakra is balanced:

Do I accept myself as I am?
Am I able to show compassion to others?
Do I give love unconditionally with no thought of self?
Am I content in my own company?
Do I value my closest relationships?
Do I accept people for whom they are, warts and all?

Am I loved?
Do I love myself?
Do I forgive myself?
Can I forgive others?

The more 'yes' answers to the above the more likely it is your Heart Chakra is balanced.

If your Heart Chakra is blocked, you might: Go for a walk in nature; arrange a romantic date with your partner (no matter how long you've been together); be open about your emotions; practice acceptance; carry green or pink gemstones (i.e. jade, green calcite, rhodonite or rose quartz) in your pocket or wallet.

Throat Chakra and Intuition

The Throat Chakra is located at your throat, near the Adam's Apple. This Chakra is associated with communication and expressing your 'inner truth'. When your Throat Chakra is balanced, intuitive words and thoughts will pop into your mind seemingly out of nowhere. You are given the opportunity to accept and act on this information. When your Throat Chakra is blocked you may consciously choose to ignore these insights and in turn you are disregarding your own truth. A blocked Throat Chakra can cause negative thoughts, doubts and an inability to express your true thoughts and feelings.

Questions to ask yourself to check this Chakra is balanced:

Do I find it easy to express my thoughts and feelings?
Am I a good listener?
Do I enjoy being creative?
Am I honest and truthful?
Am I able to express my inner self through art, photography, poetry or writing?
Do I make good use of my time?

Do I listen to my intuitive voice?

The more 'yes' answers to the above the more likely it is your Throat Chakra is balanced.

If your Throat Chakra is blocked, you might: Sing in the shower; express your feelings through art and creative work; arrange a heart-to-heart with your best friend or partner; attend spiritual events; Carry blue gemstones (i.e. blue calcite, blue lace agate, turquoise) in your pocket or wallet.

Third Eye Chakra and Intuition

Your Third Eye Chakra, located in the middle of your forehead, is associated with your sixth sense. This Chakra strengthens your intuitive links and clairvoyant ability. When your Third Eye Chakra is balanced, your intuition can play a strong role in your decision making. As your brain processes information it might compare similarities in current experiences with past experiences that are filed deep within your subconscious, bringing flashes of insight which your logical mind may not understand. These are gifts from your subconscious mind, should you wish to act on them. When this Chakra is blocked, you may be overly imaginative, feel disoriented, have trouble sleeping and there is a tendency to escape into a world of fantasy.

Questions to ask yourself to check this Chakra is balanced:

Am I able to turn imaginative thoughts into reality?
Do I enjoy using my imagination?
Is there a balance between logical thinking and fantasy?
Do I enjoy learning?
Am I able to gain knowledge yet still leave myself open to learning?
Am I open-minded?
Do I try to be flexible in my thinking?

Do I trust my intuition?

The more 'yes' answers to the above the more likely it is your Third Eye Chakra is balanced.

If your Third Eye Chakra is blocked, you might: Try guided meditations; start a dream journal; ask your Spirit Guides or the Universe a question and be prepared to patiently wait for the answer; carry dark blue or dark purple gemstones (i.e. indigo blue, lapis lazuli, celestite) in your pocket or wallet.

Crown Chakra and Intuition

When your Crown Chakra is balanced, you might receive premonitions that cannot be explained but which you later observe, do occur. There is a sense of 'knowing' what is about to come before it has happened. Another way your intuition works through your Crown Chakra is when you find yourself on a lucky streak: able to consistently enjoy fortunate, winning experiences despite the odds against this. Your Crown Chakra helps keep your intuition-filters clear to connect you with the Divine.

Questions to ask yourself to check this Chakra is balanced:

Am I spiritual?
Do I feel in touch with my Higher Self?
Do I have a strong sense of purpose?
Do I count my blessings regularly?
Do I meditate regularly to help me connect with the Divine?
Do I feel a strong connection with my Guides/Angels/Universal energy?
Do I feel at one with the Universe?
Am I an Old Soul?

The more 'yes' answers to the above the more likely it is your Crown Chakra is balanced.

If your Crown Chakra is blocked, you might: Turn off the TV and computer and enjoy a few hours of complete silence; connect with your inner self through contemplation and meditation; sign up on a yoga course; meditate regularly to strengthen your intuition; carry a purple gemstone (i.e. amethyst) in your pocket or wallet. Listen to classical music.

Your Palm Chakra

There are a number of minor Chakras in our hands (one at each finger, one at each thumb, one at the wrist joint and one in the palm of our hands.) These, along with many other minor Chakras, work with the seven main Chakras. Healers use their palm Chakras to help channel energy to the person they are healing and many people who work with Reiki energy will feel their hands tingle as they give healing.

When a part of our body is injured, we instinctively cover it with our hands. If a child comes to us after hurting themselves, we will reach out and hold, pat or stroke the area that hurts. We are intuitively sending healing to the injured area. Our palm Chakras can also help stimulate other Chakras. For instance, if we're struggling to communicate, we might gently cover our throat with our hands to help us express ourselves more easily. If we're upset and feeling strong emotions, covering our Heart Chakra with our palms can help soothe our emotions. If we are working on our psychic development, we might hold our palms at our Third Eye.

How to Balance Your Chakras

* Lie down in a comfortable position with a pillow under your knees to take the strain off your lower back.
* Place your left hand over your third-eye Chakra and the other over your crown Chakra.

* Close your eyes, breathe slowly and open yourself up to receiving Divine or Universal energy. Imagine a white light of energy flowing down through the top of your head, through your heart Chakra, down through your body and out through your feet.
* Take several minutes over this until you feel it is time to change.
* Now move your right hand down to your Third Eye Chakra and the other down to your Throat Chakra. Hold this position for a while.
* Then move your left hand to your Heart Chakra and your right to your Solar Plexus Chakra. Hold this position for a while, then just keep switching your hands around your Chakras at random for as long as you desire.

The above Chakra exercise will help you trust your feelings and intuition.

Psychic Workout ... Feeling the Energy

This exercise will help you 'feel' energy with your palms.
First shake your hands.
Now hold your hands out in front of you and rub them vigorously together.
Next slowly start to separate your hands ... just a few centimetres. Feel the warmth between them like a ball of energy.
Slowly bring your hands further apart. Can you still feel the energy?
Bring them back together, stretch them further apart and all the while playing with the energy between them.
If you don't feel any energy go back to the start and try again. It can take a while to feel the energy and open the Chakras in your palm so keep practising.

How to 'Feel' another Person Intuitively

Once you have practised the above exercise and can feel the energy between your palms, you might try this with another person. This can help you intuitively pick up information that might be helpful to them.

Ground and protect (see chapter 2).

Ask your Guides/Angels that anything you receive intuitively will be for the highest good of all.

Ask your volunteer to sit upright on a chair.

Now place one palm on either side of their head at their ears (you don't have to touch their head to do this)

Stay with this for some minutes, just holding your hand there and focus on connecting intuitively with your volunteer.

Make a note of anything that comes into your mind ... words, colours, images, feelings, sounds, smells.

You might speak these out loud or discuss them afterwards.

Make notes of this exercise and feedback received in your Journal.

Intuition and your Third Eye Chakra

With this Chakra being the key to intuition, I want to focus a little more on this now.

Your Third Eye Chakra is located at the centre of the forehead. This Chakra is associated with your spiritual journey and wisdom, dreams, visions, your subconscious, soul memories and insight. This Chakra is all about seeing, both with your physical eyes and intuitively. This is the Chakra that can open the door to the subconscious, to memories buried deep inside. It can help in your meditations, guiding your inner journeys and linking you to Universal energy.

The colour of this Chakra is indigo or different shades of dark blue. Indigo helps connect us to our higher selves and our intuition as well as enhancing spiritual and unconditional love.

Your Third Eye Chakra is associated with your intuitive abilities: your inner eye, inner seeing, inner knowing, inner sensing, inner hearing and inner feeling. It is the energy centre of creative visualisation, imagination and intuition.

When your Third Eye Chakra is open, you are very much aware of your inner self and in touch with your intuition. You will be highly perceptive with a heightened sense of clairvoyance. When this Chakra is closed or blocked, you may not feel or hear messages your subconscious is sending you through your dreams, flashes of inspiration or sudden thoughts. You are closed to the signs around you that might help guide you on your spiritual journey. You might feel confused, low or depressed. You may have no sense of purpose. A blocked Third Eye Chakra can show in symptoms such as insomnia, problems with hearing/ears, skin disorders, dizziness, headaches or a longing for greater balance within and in your life.

Your intuition and inner perception isn't just about sensing what's ahead but it is mostly about being able to sense the truth about yourself and others.

There are many benefits to be reaped from having your Third Eye open and receptive. These include along with enhanced intuition, being more perceptive, more imaginative, more able to remember and to benefit from your dreams. You are likely to gain in wisdom and may notice enhanced memory skills.

When your Third Eye is open and receptive you will become more in tune with what you want out of life, with your true purpose and spiritual goals. You will value the importance of intuition and imagination and you will learn to trust your instincts.

Here are some great ways to help keep the energy in your Third Eye Chakra flowing:

Meditate: Meditation is the most important method of developing intuition, psychic ability and Chakra balancing.

Be creative: draw, doodle, enjoy art, photography, poetry or writing. This helps to decrease the analytical thoughts going through your mind and stops you from over-thinking. Over-thinking can block your mental entrance to your intuition. By being creative, meditating, relaxing, taking a soothing bath or a walk you are helping to make your mind more receptive to intuitive guidance.

Don't get competitive: The intuitive mind is not competitive. The more intuitive you are, the more likely you are to avoid competitive environments. Whether in your social life, in work, in play or in education, being competitive drains your intuitive side while feeding your ego. Let go of competition and go with the flow.

Get in touch with your emotions: Put some time aside to listen to music, relax and get in touch with your emotional side. Sometimes we can go through life without acknowledging how we really feel about our relationships, activities, work and other aspects of our life. Sometimes we deliberately shut off from our emotions because we know we won't like or don't want to face what we see. When you hide from your emotions or are reluctant to express your feelings for fear of how other people might react, this is hiding your truth and damaging your true value. Your emotions deserve to be recognised, acknowledged and brought to light. It is healthy to express your feelings both to yourself and to others. Take time to sit with your emotions and recognise your true feelings.

Ask the Universe a Question – If you don't already do so, start talking to your Guides and Angels or the Universe (whatever your beliefs). Ask the Universe/your Guides a question and then wait patiently to receive the answer. The answer may come from outside (something you see, hear or receive) or it will come from within … an intuitive feeling, or through a dream for instance. You might receive the answer immediately or it may take a few weeks or even months before you know this question has been answered.

Keep notes in your Journal of any hunches, visions, feelings, strange smells or sounds that might come to you each day. Don't dismiss any of this as being silly. Be accepting as you open up to your intuitive responses. Keeping a spiritual journey is also a good way to help keep your Third Eye Chakra open and receptive. If you don't already do so, start keeping a dream journal.

Affirmations: Repeat the following affirmations whenever you feel you need to: "I am open to receiving intuitive information." "My imagination is powerful." "My mind is clear and versatile." "I am ready to gain greater spiritual awareness."

Work with your Intuition: Find a quiet place and make yourself comfortable. Now relax by focusing on your breathing. Count one as you inhale and exhale on the count of two. Once you are relaxed, think of a situation you would like more insight about. Focus on this situation, the people involved, the circumstances and or the place for a few minutes. Now ask for an intuitive experience relating to the situation in the near future. Open your eyes and let this question go. Put it out of your mind until you receive the intuitive information you requested.

Enhancing your Inner Vision: Quietly sit for a few minutes relaxing. Focus your attention on your eyebrows and forehead and feel this area relaxing. Focus for a few moments on your breathing then bring your attention back to the middle of your forehead. With your inner eye, imagine that you radiate with a glowing white light of health and happiness and feel your love touching all those who are around you.

Psychic Workout ... Your Intuitive Self: A Meditation

Find a quiet place.
Light a candle or incense stick.
Ground and Protect.
Breathe in and out slowly four times focusing on your breathing.
Feel your mind calm.
Keep focusing on your breathing as you quieten your mind.
Try to blank your mind.
When thoughts creep in, say to yourself 'vanish ... vanish' until it is calm.
Now think of a place that is meaningful to you – a holiday memory, a favourite place, a place you have always wanted to visit.
Hold this place/memory in your mind.
Imagine stepping into this place. Allow your thoughts to wander.
What can you see, hear, feel, smell, taste?
Stay here for a while. Savour the experience.
Return to normal and write this down in your Journal.
Interpret all you saw in your meditation as you would interpret a dream – what did each image, feeling, sound, smell, mean to you? If someone appeared in your meditation, what do you think of when you think of them? How did you feel while doing this meditation?

What should you do now?

Once begun, keep up your exercises to open your Third Eye Chakra but always be sure to close it after meditations and exercises by visualising the eyelid on your Third Eye closing or imagining the petals of a flower on your forehead, at the location of your Third Eye, closing.

Points to Ponder

Think about the methods you have started using to open your Third Eye Chakra. In your Psychic Journal write down the methods you intend to use in the future to make working on your Third Eye Chakra a regular experience.

Four

Crystals that enhance Intuition

How do use crystals and gemstones to become more in tune with your spiritual self

Crystals are a gentle yet effective way of helping us to balance on many levels. They work by realigning our Chakras and they help us release and work through any fears and behaviours that no longer serve us. Gemstones and crystals work on a physical, emotional, psychological and etheric level.

Working with specific crystals can enhance your intuition and help you develop a stronger link between your conscious and subconscious minds.

The word intuition comes from the Latin word 'intueri' which means to 'look upon' ... to look upon a situation immediately without using analysis or logic. It means to look inside and trust that unconscious 'knowing'. The more you trust your intuition, the more this sense of knowing will strengthen. An intuitive response is an instant and strong sense of what is happening and working with crystals can help you develop this sense.

Let us look at some of the crystals that are beneficial to enhancing intuition. If you keep ones you are drawn to, in the environment around you: in your bedroom, living room or workplace or wear them as jewellery, you might notice that you become more in tune with your intuition, your imagination and more aware of the instant and intuitive thoughts that come into your head. Trusting these instantaneous thoughts and feelings can aid you on your journey through life and can also help you develop your psychic powers.

So, when you start to feel these instant sensations (whether it is physical like goose bumps, sudden tension in your body, a heaviness in your heart or a sudden feeling like someone is not to be trusted or a certain road should be avoided) don't dismiss these feelings. Instead focus your awareness on the thought and consider whether it is linked with an aspect of your life and whether you should trust it and go with what you feel it is telling you.

There are many crystals that can help you develop your intuition and some have other qualities which might also help in your psychic development and communication with your Higher Self or spirit world.

AGATE HOLLY BLUE: This violet blue stone is one of the rarer agates. It works on the Crown, Third Eye and Heart Chakras. It has the highest vibration of all the agates. It stimulates psychic abilities by activating the psychic centres in the brain aiding ESP, Lucid dreaming and Mediumship. It helps us to 'hear' the prompting of our Guides.

AMETHYST: Amethyst is a powerfully protective crystal. It can help encourage inner strength and relieve stress. The healing energy of Amethyst can change lower vibrations to higher frequencies, turning negative energy to positive, loving energy. Amethyst connects the physical with the spiritual realm, making this a good gemstone for working with the Third Eye Chakra. It also has a peaceful energy which is good for meditation and helping to develop intuitive and psychic abilities.

ANGELITE: Angelite helps to promote inner peace and serenity and brings a sense of calm. Angelite can help us connect with our intuition and also encourages forgiveness.

AZURITE: A rare crystal that can help control the flow of energies through our Chakras. Azurite is a blue stone that stimulates communication skills, inspiration, creativity and intuition.

BLOODSTONE: Heightens intuitive ability as well as being a grounding stone.

CARNELIAN: A gemstone that will help encourage you to trust your intuition and natural psychic gifts. Carnelian can also enhance clairvoyant and clairaudient abilities and is a good stone to choose for psychic protection.

CELESTITE: A good choice to help with meditation as Celestite helps us block out distracting noise and focus our minds. This pale blue, sparkly gemstone has a peaceful energy and is connected with Angelic realms. As well as helping to calm and focus your mind it has the additional quality of helping to develop patience and understanding.

CLEAR QUARTZ: Balances conscious mind with subconscious. Helps with emotional healing. Clarifies mind and focuses thoughts and energy. This is an easy, reasonably priced crystal to find and is often recommended for intuitive and psychic development. Clear quartz can help amplify your intuitive senses and align you with your spiritual purpose.

DUMORTIERITE: Activates the Third Eye and stimulates psychic and mental abilities, emotional intelligence and is supportive of psycchometry and psychokinesis. Great for mental discipline and memory retention. – Ideal for those working with Astrology and Tarot.

HEMATITE: Hematite is a good grounding stone. It can help calm the mind, decrease negativity, reduce stress and bring a greater awareness of personal issues and patterns.

KYANITE: Kyanite helps bring hidden truths to the surface. It is a good stone to choose when doing dreamwork as it helps to make our dreams more vivid and makes it easier for us to recall our dreams. Kyanite can also create a bridge between ourselves and our Guides so they can come through more easily in our dreams. It can be used, too, to remove negative energies.

LAPIS LAZULI: Helps to enhance our inner power, intuition and imagination.

MALACHITE: Malachite can help bring psychic visions. Its spiritual energy can also help us remember our dreams.

MOONSTONE: Calms emotions, brings inspiration and enhances intuition.

PYRITE: Enhances creativity and mental stability Blocks negativity and is a powerful protection stone.

PYROMORPHITE: Works on Solar Plexus and Heart Chakras. Enhances intuition of the physical and spiritual bodies giving accurate 'gut feelings' about people and situations. Helps calm anger and release negative thoughts. Allows you to tolerate toxic people around you, to a degree, without being detrimentally affected.

SHAMAN STONE: This circular sandstone from Utah is great for Shamanic journeying and deep inner work. It also stimulates all Chakras.

SHATTUCKITE: Works on Heart and Throat Chakras. Stimulates intuition. Good for when communicating with spirit as it will help you find the right words to pass on messages. A good stone to choose when working with tarot, runes and angel cards.

SOLADITE: This stone has a gentle energy that encourages intuitive perception while helping you to remain logical. Soladite helps to activate your Third Eye Chakra and brings trust and harmony in group work making this a good gemstone to choose while you are working with a partner in developing your intuition.

TIGER'S EYE: Tiger's eye is another gemstone that can help stimulate your Third Eye Chakra. This gemstone also has protective qualities. It can help you recognise your strengths and weaknesses.

You might carry gemstones you feel drawn to in your pocket, wallet, purse or handbag to benefit from their energies during the course of the day. You could sleep with a chosen gemstone under your pillow or keep them on your desk or a window sill in a room you spend a lot of time in. It would be best to choose one or two stones at a time rather than a mix of all otherwise the energies can get confused. Also if you choose one at a time this will help you find the gemstones that work best for you.

Psychic Workout ... Developing your Intuition with Crystals

Exercise 1: Place a number of crystals spaced out on a table in front of you. Now close your eyes and pass your left hand over the crystals. Try to feel the different energies and notice any changes like feeling warm or cold as you pass your palm over the crystals. Does any image or colour come to your mind as you do this? When this happens open your eyes to see which crystal has stimulated this image/feeling. Pick up this crystal and consider its properties and associations and how these might be of benefit to you at this particular time.

Exercise 2: With a crystal of your choice (either choose a crystal you are drawn to intuitively or choose it for its qualities as described above) find a quiet place where you won't be disturbed. Hold the crystal in your hand. Now start to focus on your breathing. As you relax allow your thoughts to go where they want. Afterwards, write down all that came to you in your Psychic Journal.

Exercise 3: For this exercise you might choose Azurite (a stone that helps to enhance communication between your conscious and subconscious mind). Carnelian (to help you trust your intuitive ability), and Lapis Lazuli or Malachite (a gemstone that can give psychic visions). Cup the crystal in your hands and ask yourself a question such as 'what do I need in life right now?' Ask the question three times and each time you will get a stronger sense of the answer. On the third question, ask for a symbol to represent the answer. Now draw this symbol in your Psychic journal. Next work on interpreting this symbol as this is an intuitive message in response to the question.

Exercise 4: With a crystal of your choice, hold the crystal in your hands and think about the people in your life that matter most to you. Ask the crystal to help you be aware of those people who help to make you happy, healthy and emotionally content. Imagine they are with you at this present time and this will help you to develop your intuitive eye.

What should you do now?

Choose three gemstones and spend some time feeling their energy. Consider their colours and shapes. Use your intuition: how does this gemstone make you feel? Does it have a calming energy, does it help you feel grounded? Does it take you to memories of the past or hopes for the future? Write down all that comes to you as you focus on the three gemstones.

Points to Ponder

A useful quote to think about:

"Intuitive impressions are subtle and can "evaporate" quickly. Neuroscience research indicates that intuitive insights not captured within thirty-seven seconds will likely never be recalled again. Many people find journal writing to be a highly effective way to access their intuition. Try it. You'll be amazed at the clarity of what comes through." - Jack Canfield

Five

Colour and Intuition

How do use colours to enhance and deepen your intuition sensing

Working with colour is a great way to enhance your intuition. Colours radiate energy, every colour having its own vibration. Tuning into colours can help unlock your intuitive power. Imagine living in a world that is only black and white and different shades of grey. – A world without colour. Life would start to feel drab and dreary. There would be no colours to stimulate mind and emotions. Colour helps to heighten our perceptions in our day to day lives and can be used as a tool in meditation and healing.

Colours stimulate our emotions. Just imagine seeing a rainbow. How does this make you feel? So many people feel hopeful and uplifted when they see a rainbow. Colours are used in signs and symbols as a silent language that communicates messages of power, war, royalty, mysticism, warnings, nationalism etc. Why, for instance is the velvet in a crown purple? ... Purple is the traditional colour of the leader of a country. In many cultures there is a strong link between the colour purple and royalty. Purple is a mix of red and blue. Red is associated with war, blood and energy. Blue is associated with law and the Throat Chakra relating to communication and truth.

Our own colours can be picked up in our auras. Some psychics can sense or see auras and auras can also be photographed.

Working with colour or visualising colour triggers our intuition and helps heal our mind, body and spirit. For example, if you visualise yourself being surrounded by pink energy, you are stimulating your heart Chakra, enhancing feelings of love and releasing memories of emotional hurt. Pink is a colour that resonates with gentle, loving and caring energy. Colour can therefore be used as an intuitive form of healing. Green is a colour that helps promote good health. Blue can produce a serene mood and helps relieve tension.

Intuitive Colour Healing

"Colours, like feathers, follow the changes of the emotions" ...
Pablo Picasso

Rainbow Healing involves alternative therapies using colour as a
form of healing of mind, body, emotions and spirit.

For so many people, simply observing a rainbow in all its glory
can be a powerfully uplifting experience. Tuning into the various
colours of the rainbow for healing can be extremely relaxing as
well as helping to reconnect a person with their Higher Self.

Practitioners of Rainbow Healing draw on the psychology and
history of colour and how colours relate to the Chakras, to bring
comfort and healing. They might also use other spiritual tools
such as crystals, aromatherapy and pendulum dowsing within the
healing session.

How do colours help restore the energy balance within our
bodies? It has been found that different colours vibrate at
different frequencies. People automatically relate colour to
moods, for instance if someone is feeling 'blue', they may be
going through a depressed phase. Think of the phrase 'green
with envy'. This colour actually relates to the heart Chakra and
can be used to bring harmony, compassion and understanding in
healing. Too much green on the other hand might cause
jealousy, indifference and a lack of sensitivity.

Because Rainbow Therapy is all about using colours to help
balance the person within, too much of a certain colour can have
the opposite affect to what it is being used for. If, for instance,
red is over used it can promote anger and agitation.

Through Rainbow Therapy, the different colours of the rainbow
are used to stimulate and recharge energies depending on a
person's mood and physical condition. Although complex in
nature, the following gives a brief description of how colours are
used in healing:

Orange - Orange helps to strengthen the immune system and increase sexual energy. After illness, this colour can be used to help build up a person's strength. Orange is also the colour of joy and creativity associated with the Sacral Chakra. Too much Orange: An excess of Orange can cause arrogance, over-optimism and selfishness.

Red - Red helps recharge energy. It is often used for poor circulation, multiple sclerosis and anaemia and for illnesses related to the spinal column and the kidneys. Red can help increase willpower and determination and is associated with the Root Chakra. Too much Red: An excess of red can cause irritability, anger, bossiness and hyper-activity.

Blue - Blue helps bring a feeling of peace; it is a calming colour. As well as helping to bring more settled emotions, blue is the colour that might be chosen for feverish conditions, nausea, an underactive thyroid and lung problems. Blue helps communication, awakens intuition and is associated with the Throat Chakra. Too much Blue: An excess of Blue can cause arrogance, hyperactivity, depression and negativity.

Indigo - Purple helps balance all the energies in the aura; it might be used in meditation and to help cure headaches. Indigo enhances clairvoyance and intuition and is associated with the Third Eye Chakra. Too much Indigo: An excess of Indigo can cause ego to get into the way of spiritual development.

Violet - Violet helps to inspire and purify. This colour may be used to restore a person's perspective and to help balance mind, body and emotions. It might also be used for cancer, arthritis, sciatica, neuralgia and bladder problems. Too much Violet: An excess of Violet can cause suppressed anger and aggravation.

Yellow - Yellow helps lift the spirit and clears the mind. This colour is often used to help give those who are depressed or stressed a mental uplift. Yellow in healing might be chosen for stomach upsets, bladder problems and loss of appetite. Yellow helps focus the mind and enhances optimism. This colour is associated with the Solar Plexus Chakra. Too much Yellow: An excess of Yellow can cause restlessness, confusion and stubbornness.

Green - Green is a powerfully healing colour, relating to the Heart Chakra. It might be used for high blood pressure, stress related illnesses, the heart and circulatory system and to promote calmness. Green enhances feeling of love, compassion and empathy. Too much Green: An excess of Green can cause jealousy, miserliness and over confidence.

Rainbow Therapists draw on the effects of colour to help heal the body and soul. An awareness of how colour resonates with your own wavelengths may help attract more joy, passion and happiness into your life and enhance your good health.

Psychic Workout ... Colour Intuitive Exercise

How does colour affect your mood?

Colours give off a vibration and this vibration can affect our mood, our thoughts and even our health. So, how do you respond to colour? Here is a list of colours. Alongside each colour write down what qualities, characteristics and feelings come to you when you think of that colour.

Remember, everyone is different so one colour might mean one thing to you but something quite different to another person. What do these colours mean to you?

Blue / Green / Red / Yellow / Grey / White / Ivory / Brown
Pink / Gold / Silver / Purple / Beige / Black / Orange

Colours and Environment

The main colours of a room, office or the workplace can evoke emotional responses. Research into colour has found that colours don't only affect mood but can have an impact on productivity. With this in mind, think about the main places you spend your time in, the colour schemes of these areas and how these might affect your own moods.

Researchers at Creighton University in Omaha found that colours painted on office walls influenced workers' emotions and efficiency. Employees in blue offices, for instance, felt calm, hopeful about their work and most centred.

How might the colour of your environment affect your mood, productivity and stress levels?

Red increases physical energy and can make you more productive. Red can stimulate creativity but also anger and impatience.

Yellow enhances positivity and optimism. It aids concentration but too much yellow can cause ill-temper. Babies have been found to cry more in a yellow room.

Orange encourages sociability.

Blue reduces stress and encourages stability and ability to communicate. Blue stimulates the mind.

Brown enhances practicality and brings a sense of stability and order.

Green is calming and refreshing. Green helps relax and is a good colour to choose for healing environments.

What should you do now?

This exercise will help you feel the energy of different colours, sensing their qualities and your emotional responses as they travel through your body.

Find an object with a specific colour to focus on such as a red flower, green leaf, black gemstone. Now relax and fill your mind with this colour. Visualise this colour moving down from the crown of your head into your body. Note how you feel as you imagine this colour filling you from head to toe. Write your feelings in your Journal.

Work your way through as many colours as you can find.

Points to Ponder

Think about the colours you use when decorating your space, about how you want to feel (relaxed, studious, creative, for instance) and how you want others to feel when they visit. How might existing colours affect your mood and the emotive response of visitors?

Six

Listen to your Intuition

How do you listen to your intuition?

In this day and age when there is so much happening around us, we are surrounded by technology and life seems to get faster and faster it isn't always easy to listen to our inner voice. The more in tune you are with your intuition, the easier it will be to tune into it even when in noisy surroundings. But at first, when learning to listen to your intuition, it helps if you can make time to be quiet and to still your mind.

To listen to your inner voice, turn off the TV, mobile phone and computer. Find quiet surroundings where you won't be distracted by the noises around you so you can focus on your inner ear. When all is quiet, close your eyes and just allow your mind to turn inwards. Let your thoughts flow to wherever they might take you. If your mind feels too cluttered, imagine a blackboard (chalkboard) in front of you and watch as it is completely erased. Now your mind is clear and this can help you listen to your inner voice.

You might spend time alone in nature and notice how the sounds of nature make you feel deep inside. ... Notice the scents around you and what feelings or memories they might stir.

Your time is precious. So why waste it on worrying about what other people think or trying to live someone else's life rather than focusing on your own? Are you allowing other people to do all the talking and is this drowning out your inner voice? How can you follow your heart if you don't spend quiet time tuning into your inner thoughts?

Set your mind free from making judgements or any kind of prejudice. Let your spirit fly.

Reconnect with your body and LISTEN to your gut feeling. If for instance you are about to do something or you hear something and your stomach lurches and feels heavy, this could be a warning. On the other hand if you feel a warm, glowing sensation inside, this could be your intuition telling you a situation is right for you or to go for it. If you suddenly get a lump in your throat or your throat goes dry and you feel nervous, this can be instinct warning you that something isn't right. Different people have different ways of tuning into their inner voice and sensing the way their body communicates with them intuitively.

LISTEN to your heart. When you feel confused and uncertain you might turn to other people for advice. This can add to your confusion because not everyone will give you the same advice and not everyone knows you as well as you should know yourself. If you're trying to make a decision that affects YOUR future, why rely on others to make it for you? Instead make a list of pros and cons. Consider the list. Give yourself time to let it all sink in and then return to it. – What is the first thing that jumps out at you. Let the answer come from your heart and not from other people.

LISTEN to your Dreams: Dreams can be a great source of self-analysis and the more we work with our dreams, the more in touch we become with our inner selves. Dreams can help us understand our feelings towards events and people and what we are going through. Dreams can give a glimpse into the future, enhance our creativity, reinforce what we have learned and help us solve problems. Dreams open the door to our spiritual selves.

When we enter the world of dreams, we see images or a series of images played out through the lens of our Third Eye. These images are like our own personal show or cinema screen, showing us stories or snapshots of our inner life. By remembering our dreams and analysing their content we can explore our inner selves and enhance the relationship between our conscious mind and our subconscious.

This is a technique that can be used to answer a question through your dreams or to provide information which is hidden from the conscious mind. This exercise is best carried out just before going to sleep.

• Take a relaxing bath. Add a few drops of Jasmine or Rose essential oils to aid creative dreaming.
• After your bath, light a pink or lilac candle in your bedroom
• Write down the question you need answering or a problem that is on your mind
• As you sit in the candlelight, read the question out loud.
 • Blow out the candle. Repeat the question once more. Allow it to drift into the smoke of the extinguished candle.
• Set your intention to have a good night's sleep and to remember your dreams on waking
• You may not get a direct answer from your dreams but if you start keeping a dream journal you might start noticing clues or you may find your mind drifts towards the answer triggered by something you saw in a dream.

Psychic Workout … Developing your Intuition

Find a shallow dish and fill it with water. Draw shapes on the water with your finger. This will help relax you and focus your thoughts on the water. Now watch as the shapes change and the water ripples. What feelings come to you? What images? Write these down in your journal. – You can also add a little bubble bath or washing up liquid to the water and see what you can see in the water.

Intuition and Animals

Animals rely on instinct in order to survive. Some people have exceptional talents in tuning in to animals to understand and communicate with them. We might use our intuition to communicate with animals. For instance, although my dog showed no outer sign of being distressed, I began to worry that she was ill. To me, she wasn't 'right in herself' and this concerned me so much that I took her to the vets. She was wagging her tail and seemed fine with the vet but because of my concerns the vet gave her a scan and discovered she had pyometra and needed an operation immediately because of the infection already in her body. Had I not went to the vets she could have died of toxaemia. Fortunately, I had an understanding vet who actually told me he found that pet owners had an intuitive feeling about their pets that nine times out of ten proved correct.

Exercise: Animal Spirits

Have you noticed how sometimes you might see the same animal cropping up again and again? For instance you might see a butterfly as you're walking to work then as you look out the window during your tea-break, you notice a butterfly at the window. Or you might switch on the TV and there is a documentary about elephants and then you might notice a magazine article on elephants or a painting of elephants in a shop window. Have you ever asked yourself why you are suddenly noticing these and what they might mean?

Some cultures believe we have animal Guides and certain animal spirits will come into our life at a time when we need their guidance/teaching. Animal spirits can bring lessons or help us cope with experiences we are going through. There are many internet sites that will give interpretations of Animal Guides and like all symbols, an animal will mean something different for different people. So for instance a camel might mean carrying heavy burdens to one person or may be a symbol of endurance and strength to another.

Here is a list of animals. What do these mean to you? Although there are interpretations you will find on the internet giving you what different spirit animals can mean, remember that it is what a symbol means to 'you' that is important.

Dog / Cat / Rabbit / Crow / Horse / Mouse / Butterfly / Cat / Elephant / Bear / Wolf / Tiger

---

When you listen to your intuition you are listening to your best friend who is always there to guide and protect you, to inspire you and warn you. When listening to your intuition you will find answers through your dreams and you will discover you can anticipate events and trust your feelings about how things will develop.

What should you do now?

Close your eyes, relax and focus on your breathing.
Imagine you are standing in a field surrounded by trees.
Now ask to see an animal come out from the trees and into the field.
What is this animal?

Get your journal and write what comes to mind as you think of the following questions:
If this animal symbolises your intuition, what might it mean?
What are this animals characteristics?
What can you learn from considering these characteristics?

Points to Ponder

How do you listen to your intuition? ... Just write and let the words flow.

Seven

Personality and Intuition

Personality, Ego and Intuition

Psychology research has found that intuitive people show certain characteristics more strongly than in others.

Intuitive people for instance listen to their inner voice. We are all intuitive to a certain degree. Intuitive people trust the guidance that comes from within. They enjoy their own company and will make time for solitude.

Intuitive people are:

*often introverted and need silence to recharge their emotional/spiritual batteries. They are in tune with their physical-selves and heed their gut feelings.

* usually gentle, caring and complex in personality. Many intuitives are artistic, creative or musical.

* have uncanny insight into other people's personalities and situations. – They get strong feelings such as sensing a loved one is ill or in danger and later hearing the person that was on their mind was in an accident or taken to hospital.

* usually very private people. They are also good at keeping other people's secrets. They generally avoid conflict and if they must face conflict they do so from a 'feeling' angle, placing less importance on who is in the right but how the situation makes them feel. Often they will try to remove themselves in order to sort out their feelings before making decisions.

* good counsellors and mediators, helping to mediate other people's conflict as they intuitively sense how others' feel and feel a sincere desire to help them.

Anxiety and upset can block their intuition and it isn't until they step away that they feel more able to see more clearly what needs to be done.

Many intuitive people will keep these feelings to themselves because few other people understand them and therefore they are protective of their 'inner knowing,' sharing these only with those they trust.

If you are an intuitive empath, you will be sensitive to the feelings of other people and you are likely to be a good listener. You will pick up on other people's hidden emotions or suppressed feelings. Because intuitive empaths soak in the feelings, mood and atmosphere around them it is important that they protect their energy through grounding and psychic protection. It can also help to avoid negative people so as not to absorb their negative energy.

Intuitive empaths should spend time alone to reconnect with their inner selves. Intuitive empaths make good counsellors as they recognise these feelings in other people and bring them to light to help others rebalance their lives.

Are sensitive people intuitive?

A sensitive person is not necessarily intuitive. A sensitive person will pick up information through sensations such as touch, sounds, sight and other stimuli. A person who relies on their senses will make decisions based on outside influences. An intuitive person is more focused on what they 'feel' within.

Whereas a sensitive person is observant and watchful and more attentive to their surroundings, an 'intuitive' is more concerned with what they pick up instinctively. If you watch the eyes of a sensitive person they are likely to be alert, focused and watchful whereas the eyes of an intuitive person may seem unfocused as their mind is actually focused on what's going on within rather than without.

Personality, Ego and Intuition

By now you know that intuition is not using analysis or reason. An intuitive response is an instant knowing, feeling or sensation. Some people will ask how they know an intuitive response isn't just guesswork and, really, only time will give the answer. The more you work with your intuition the more you will grow to trust it and you will just know when you should act on these feelings. If you have a big ego, you might find it more difficult to gain access to your intuitive side. Your mind will be more focused on facts and other information that you think will be useful to you.

People might act egotistically to portray more confidence than they actually have (so actually they are insecure inside) or they may act in a way that brings attention to themselves because they want to appear successful to others. Over confidence, arrogance, pride, self-importance and conceit are all qualities that can block the link between your conscious mind and your intuition. Equally if you are anxious, confused or upset, this can restrict your link with your intuitive mind.

What else can block your intuition? – People who are critical, judgemental, biased and who show prejudice aren't likely to have a high sense of intuition. Being free from judgement can help you develop your intuition.

Intuition can be cultivated by adopting a mindful, non-judgemental awareness and by allowing your intuitive side to express itself by developing empathy, sensitivity and inner tranquillity.

How can Intuition be Enhanced?

Intuition can be enhanced by calming your mind and being sensitive to your thoughts and feelings; also by being sensitive to other people's feelings and your surroundings. Be mindful of thoughts and aware of bodily sensations (shivers down the spine, gut feelings) that may be intuitive responses. Be alert to what is going on at this present moment as being observant can aid intuitive responses, so watch what is going on and listen attentively. When you listen to others your mind will also be alert to both verbal and nonverbal clues and this will help you intuitively pick up what people may not be saying in words.

Being kind, compassionate and loving towards others can help increase your sensitivity and intuitive responses.

If you lead a busy lifestyle, arrange it so you have quiet times to yourself to meditate. Try to slow down the pace of your life as this can help you take a deeper look within and at what is going on around you.

Express gratitude. Whenever you receive help from your intuition, your Spirit Guides or your Higher Self (depending on your beliefs) don't forget to say 'thank you'.

And don't forget to keep a note of all your intuitive experiences in your Journal.

Psychic Workout ... Developing Your intuition in Everyday Life

How might you develop your intuition in your daily life? You can practice using your intuition anywhere, even standing in a bus queue. Here are some ideas on how you might exercise your intuitive muscles:

1 in a bus queue .... As you watch the traffic pass, close your eyes and intuitively feel which colour the next car that passes will be when you open them.

2 when the phone rings, before answering, see if you can intuitively feel who is ringing you

3 when standing waiting for a lift/elevator, which do you think will arrive first?

4 If the doorbell rings and you aren't expecting anyone, who do you think it is?

The more you practice this, the more accurate your guesses will be.

Personality Styles and Intuition

Intuition is a part of your personality and personality is in itself complicated. No two people are ever completely alike. There are different personality types to which intuitive people belong and again, someone might recognise a little of one type and a little of another, as resonating with themselves.

We have already discussed being an Intuitive Empath. – Intuitive Empaths are acutely sensitive. They might find themselves feeling overwhelmed in crowded situations and will prefer being on their own or with a small group of people to being in large social gatherings. Intuitive Empaths can also be hypersensitive to scents, noise and loud conversations.

Extraverted Intuitives can pick up on how all things in life are connected. They see new possibilities and can intuit the possible consequences of decisions and actions. They are in tune with the environment around them and strive to make positive changes and instigate improvements. They have an entrepreneurial mindset and can become restless for change. Extraverted intuitives will take an instinctive response to experiences and will welcome new challenges with enthusiasm.

Introverted Intuitives sense or feel possibilities and patterns. They prefer to work in the background and will intuitively make sense of factual information. They aren't so much interested in facts but with ideas, theories and patterns. Intuition might speak to these people through their creativity ... through their ability to create.

Psychic Workout ... Colours, Numbers and Intuition

This exercise involves using your intuition to guess which colour or number another person is thinking of.

Find a friend to join in with this exercise or practice this on Social Networking sites or you might text each other.

Decide whether you want to start with a colour or number. If choosing a number keep it between 1-10 to start with. Focus on sending that mental image to whoever you are paired with. Imagine the colour or number being sent through a beam of pure white light to the recipient. When you think you have the answer reveal it to your partner then your partner takes their turn.

Remember to centre yourself first with some deep breaths and imagine yourself being filled with light.

What should you do now?

Make a heading in your Journal: 'Not all highly sensitive people are introverts' and write down your feelings on this subject.

Points to Ponder

Describe some traits associated with intuitive people and how some personality traits and emotions can block intuition.

Eight

How your Relationships can have an effect on your Intuition

How relationships can influence intuition and intuition can influence relationships

There are many types of people in this world. Some are caring, kind and giving, others will take what they can from relationships and move on. These toxic types know how kind people will go to great lengths to make those they care about happy, and they will take advantage of this.

If you have friends that continue to take without giving, stop trying to please them. If your efforts to make others happy or to bring a balance of caring and sharing into your relationship do not work, or they don't last very long, ask yourself whether it is time to walk away. Remember that you are not responsible for another person's happiness, or their behaviour.

Toxic people will surround you with constant chaos and will make you tense and miserable. Their demands and negative energy will eventually pull you into their disorder, blocking your intuitive responses and belief in yourself. You might find yourself having to constantly defend yourself against their accusations or trying to find reasons in your mind why you are remaining in a relationship that isn't bringing you any happiness.

Let your intuition guide you away from this person as they will not change. Allow your intuition to steer you clear of people and situations that might harm you in the long-term.

Do you get overwhelmingly exhausted at parties and large social gatherings? Do you wonder how some people leave groups looking animated and full of energy when you always leave feeling tired, drained and sometimes even with odd aches and pains that weren't there previously? - If so you are empathic. Not only do you absorb other people's moods, emotions, and pain but you come away from such situations uncertain of what emotions are 'yours' and which ones you've absorbed into your aura from others.

You may for instance find that some people's company can be really draining, leaving you feeling mentally and emotionally exhausted. They might seem to part from you smiling and as you watch them go you're left feeling strangely heavy and confused about your thoughts, feelings and even beliefs.

As an empath you are particularly vulnerable to emotional vampires. These are people who will constantly talk about themselves, their problems, their grievances, their hurts and their pains. They thrive on attention and drain the energy of those around them because of their need for constant feedback ... and for their starving ego to be continually fed.

Their excessive need for validation, feedback and attention will drain your energy.

Emotional Vampires:

*Draw attention to themselves ... constantly
* Will do anything or say anything to turn the focus away from others and bring it back to themselves
* Are very demanding of your time especially when they are feeling depressed and miserable
* Demand constant feedback and validation
* Complain about people not listening to them when in fact that's all that other people do
* Feel as if life is never fair to them
* Feel as if no one understands them
* Feel as if life is unfair to them
* Are argumentative
* Throw tantrums when they don't get their own way
* Blame other people or 'life' for their problems – it is never their fault
* Have needs that are always more important than other people's

If you recognise this person among your friends, try to turn attention away from them. Move your own focus to positive people. (You can sense relaxed, upbeat people if you are an empath).

How to Protect yourself against Emotional / Spiritual Vampires:

* Ground and protect (see chapter two) before meeting with people and especially when likely to go out in crowds
* Keep your own thoughts and feelings to yourself (never confide in an Emotional Vampire)
* Set a limit to how much time you spend listening to their tales of woe: after listening for a few minutes, make an excuse to leave
* Stay calm and don't react if they deliberately try to provoke you or upset you

Spend time with positive friends and people whose company is uplifting. People you mix with can make a huge difference to your life. Negative people will bring you down too, eventually. Remember, you can only do 'so much' to help others especially those who won't help themselves. You might be a positive person but if you have a friend who is always miserable, no matter how hard you try to inspire them to be cheerful, eventually they will drag your mood down to. Of course, there will be times when you will want to try to help friends who are going through hard times, but limit how much attention you give them to protect your 'self'.

If you get up every morning to be greeted by a grumpy partner, no matter what your mood at the start of the day, how are you likely to feel? You might wonder why, when you woke up feeling refreshed and hopeful about what the day ahead might bring, you quickly started to feel negative and miserable. – You have unconsciously soaked up the negative vibes from others around you. Can you imagine what this will do to you living with such a person, day after day? Eventually you won't know which feelings are your own and which are theirs. You might see yourself as being a rather negative person when in fact you are soaking in the moods of the surly people around you.

Rather than spending time with negative friends, start to focus on positive people instead.

The people you mix with can either drain your energy and leave you feeling as miserable as they happen to be, or they can uplift and inspire you as you can inspire them … whose company will you choose now?

Personalities and Intuition

Some people are naturally in tune with their intuition and feminine side. These people are likely to be spiritual, creative, imaginative and sensitive.

Some people are pragmatic and practical and will say they won't believe anything unless they 'see it with their own eyes'. There are people who respect the views and feelings of others; there are people who can only see life through their own eyes.

Controlling people may try to convince you that it isn't sensible or realistic to trust your intuition. They will use a variety of methods to dent your confidence in your intuition. When seeds of doubt are planted in your mind, you may start to listen more to such friends and less to your Higher Self. At times like these you may have to take yourself off on your own to reconnect with your inner-you.

Watch out for people who will:
* Charm you into thinking their way is the right way
* Manipulate you into feeling indebted or obligated to them in some way (i.e. doing you favours when you hadn't asked for them or being overly nice to you)
* Make their views sound more believable than yours or use their powers of persuasion to talk you out of trusting your intuitive responses
* Insult you by making fun of the trust you have in your intuition until you start doubting it yourself
* Promise you that they know best when in fact there is no guarantee their decisions or choices will be any more successful than yours

---

Psychic Workout ... Recognising your Intuitive Responses

Your intuitive response is the FIRST RESPONSE that comes into your mind before anything else. The moment your mind starts to reason and analyse, you might dismiss the instinctive response – your gut instinct – only to find later you should have trusted your hunches.

To understand this, look at the following words and write down the FIRST THING that comes into your head ... follow this by any subsequent thoughts.

Am I happy?
What makes me sad?
What makes me joyful?
Am I fulfilled?
What is my soul's purpose?
What makes my life complete?
Who causes me most problems?
What causes me most problems?
What should I be doing next?
Favourite memory?
Am I true to myself?
What is my strength?
What is my weakness?
Who do I love?
Do I feel loved?
Do I trust my intuition?
Do I listen to my intuition?
Do I act on my intuition?

Now look at your answers. The first thing that came to you instantly on seeing the words will have been your intuitive response. All later responses will have been influenced by your conscious mind.

Feeling other People's Energy

I have already mentioned our Palm Chakras. Through our hands we touch and feel objects in the world around us and other people. Intuitive people can pick up energy from the world through their palms. When we meet people we might shake hands; we 'extend the hand of friendship' and in so doing we are also directing our energy towards someone and receiving their energy through this connection.

If you are 'sensitive' to other people's energy, don't be surprised if after shaking someone's hands you have a sense of the person ... you might instinctively feel they are a 'good' person, you can trust them or there is something about them that makes you a little wary.

How can Intuition affect or influence Relationships?

Following your gut instinct can be as simple as trusting your first impressions when meeting someone. You might for instance get a feeling someone can't be trusted when you are introduced. Following your intuition can help keep you safe.

You may, for reasons you can't quite understand, get a strange feeling on a first date. You might get a bad vibe from someone or just a feeling that they aren't right for you and something will tell you this isn't a relationship you should encourage.

Many people who meet 'the one' will just know, the moment they are introduced, that this is the person for them. How do they know? This is their instinctive response to an instant bond that sparks something special deep inside.

Some friendships feel 'right' from the start and you get a good sensation from them. Others, you know deep down, aren't right for you. – Again, this is your inner voice letting you know, often before you can understand why, that this is a relationship that is unlikely to last.

What should you do now?

Put some time aside to reflect on your close relationships and friendships. Now make a list in your journal of the main people in your life. Beside each name write the first word that comes into your mind when you think of this relationship. Once you've done this consider the relationships and the word you have used intuitively to describe them.

Points to Ponder

Why not share emails or conversations with any of your spiritual friends discussing some of your intuitive experiences and asking them to share similar experiences of your own? This will help you recognise your own intuitive responses. You might also think about how other people understand and respond to their intuition and the different types of life experiences in which you and others rely on your intuition.

Nine

Developing your Intuition

How can different 'tools', techniques and routines help enhance intuition?

Tools and Intuition

We use the word 'tools' when applied to psychic development as the use of anything that helps us tune into our intuition. In this final chapter, we will look at how different 'tools', techniques, attitudes and routines can help enhance intuition.

Oracle Cards: There are many different types of Oracle Cards available. Oracle Cards help you to link with your intuition to receive guidance in daily issues, insight into problems you're trying to solve, or help with spiritual and personal development.

Pendulums/Dowsing: When using a pendulum, you are accessing information from your Higher Self. Pendulums give an answer we can see with our eyes (depending on the swing of the pendulum) that responds to what our intuition already knows.

Doodles: It can be amazing what you can 'see' in doodles if you look with your inner eye. While listening to music or sitting relaxing, draw a doodle. Now take a deeper look at the doodle. What symbols do you pick up within? What do these 'say' to you intuitively?

Tarot Cards: Images on tarot cards trigger intuitive responses to help you receive messages from the Divine/Universe/your Higher Self.

Dreams: Dreams can provide answers to everyday problems, solutions to difficulties we are going through, insight into our personalities and creative inspiration.

Objects: Through 'touch' we can pick up energy from objects (psychometry) and intuitively pick up information from the object that isn't apparent to our conscious mind.

Attitude to help Enhance Intuition

Positive Thinking: Through developing a positive outlook, you are giving out a positive vibration to the world. This will help you attract positive people into your life and opportunities that are good for you. The higher your energy through a positive, loving, outlook, the more likely it is that you will attract good energy your way.

Letting Go: Anxiety, worries, negative thoughts and negative feelings all block our intuition. We need to let go of negative emotions to keep our intuition flowing.

Believe in Yourself: Believe you are intuitive. Trust your hunches. Don't block your intuition through thinking you aren't intuitive.

Develop a Happy, Contented Outlook: We can't all be happy all of the time but being miserable will block your intuition. Try to see the good in others. Count your blessings. Be content with what you have. Think of those times when you have felt really happy and how this has increased your optimism and your sense that 'good things will come your way.' Happiness helps you tune into your intuition.

Trust your First Response: Remember that the very first thoughts, feelings, images that come to your mind are your intuitive responses. Trust your first response.

Routines to help enhance intuition

Meditation: Helps to calm our minds and heighten our intuition.

Keep a Journal: Use your interior monologue or stream of consciousness to just write down all the thoughts and feelings that are going through your mind. Set yourself 15 minutes to write. Don't think about grammar, punctuation or spelling; just write whatever comes into your head.

You might also choose a subject or heading such as:

* My earliest memory
* My childhood
* A person in my childhood who inspired me
* My favourite possessions
* People I have lost
* Music
* My favourite places
* My relationships with a sister or brother
* A decision I have to make
* Am I happy?

Or you might choose your own themes.

Get Creative: Creativity helps us express our thoughts and feelings and connects us with our intuition.

Go for a walk: Walking connects us with nature and also to our inner-selves as we are able to listen to our inner voice while walking. – It helps to walk alone or choose a quiet companion to walk with.

Be aware of sudden feelings: Don't dismiss sudden thoughts and feelings that pop into your mind as being insignificant. Ask yourself what the feeling might be telling you.

Pay attention to your body's reactions: If you get a gut feeling about something; if the hairs stand up on the back of your neck or you get a shiver down your spine, this is your intuition communicating with you. Trust and pay attention.

Learn from experience: Keeping a journal helps you look back on your intuitive experiences. Was there a time when you felt you had to do something, ignored it, and discovered later you should have gone with your instinct? Have you trusted your intuition and been glad you did so?

Ask a question of the Universe: When you're confused or need guidance, talk to your Spirit Guides. Ask the Divine, the Universe or whatever you believe in to help you and wait patiently for an answer. This may come from signs around you or it may come from within.

Go on a Spiritual Retreat: What more can be said? This will do your intuition the power of good.

Final Point to Ponder

"Everything I do is just really my intuition, and every time I go against my intuition, it's a mistake. Even though I may sit down and analyse and intellectualize something on paper, if I go against my gut feeling, it is wrong." ~ Tamara Mellon

Thank you for reading and for walking a little way with me on your spiritual journey,
Blessings,
Carole Anne

If you enjoyed this book, further books by this author can be found at:

Amazon.co.uk – Carole Somerville
Amazon.com – Carole Somerville

41619081R00043

Made in the USA
San Bernardino, CA
16 November 2016